Air Fryer Cookbook 2021

Amazingly Delicious and Crispy Recipes for Healthy Fried Favorites, A Wide Varieties of healthy air fryer recipes

Nichole S. Rodriguez

© Copyright 2021 - All rights reserved.

TABLE OF CONTENTS

INTRODUCTION

The secret of Air Fryer is the unique cooking technology that uses hot-air that circulates inside the fryer. It works no different than any other thermic-processing method, but without all the detrimental side-effects you get when you eat deep-fried foods, for example. You may be able not only to fry but also to bake, broil, roast, rotisserie, and steam things as well. Air Fryer can also be a great substitute for your microwave, oven, or a stove. Except it's much healthier, easier, and faster to use.

On top of that, you can use an air fryer to prepare batters and marinades. The only thing that you should never put in there is generally speaking liquids. That means that things like broth or other soups are not coming at play here. Remember, safety comes first. But given the wide variety of other things you can do with it - it's a tiny con.

Air fryer benefits

Almost no fat and oil involved

Probably the biggest benefit of using the Air Fryer is reducing the amount of oil or other fats you normally use to cook your meals. With the help of Air Fryer as much as one tablespoon is enough to gain the same effect as if you were cooking regular deep fried fries or spring rolls. As hot air circulates inside of the chamber, it makes the food crispy on the outside and tender on the inside.

Fewer calories

Needless to say, as you reduce the amount of fat in your meals, their calorific value drops as well. So not only you eat overall healthier but even your "cheat meals" are less of a problem now. As you can see, using an air fryer can effectively help you drop some extra weight. Maybe it's time you reinstated your relationship with French fries?

It's compact, and it fits everywhere

Because it takes so little space on the kitchen countertop, you don't have to worry about additional clutter. It also doesn't kill the aesthetics of your countertop. You can also put all the accessories inside the fryer, so you reduce unnecessary mess to a 0 level. See how you can start enjoying being in the kitchen again.

How to use an air fryer?

Prepare the air fryer

Some recipes will require using a basket, a rack, or a rotisserie. Some other recipes require cake or muffin pans. Before you pick the recipe and prepare your accessories, make sure they fit into your fryer.

Prepare the ingredients

Once you have all that's necessary to prepare your recipe, place the ingredients directly inside the appliance or use a basket, a rack, or a pan to do so. To prevent sticking use parchment baking paper or simply spray the food with a little bit of oil. A word of caution is necessary here. Never over-stuff the chamber with too much food. It will not cook to an equal measure, and you may find yourself getting frustrated chewing under-cooked bits. If you're planning on cooking more, multiple rounds of air-frying may be necessary.

Set the temperature and time

Many recipes will require you to control from time to time the content of your fryer while cooking. This is to make sure everything gets cooked evenly. Normally all it takes is to shake or flip the food to distribute it. For some recipes, however, you'll need to turn the food around some time halfway through the cooking.

Cleaning time

Before you start cleaning, plug the air fryer off and let it cool down. Once it's ready, stick to instructions you got from the manufacturer and never scrub or use any other abrasive material on the inner surface of the chamber.

Air fryer recipes

Keep an eye on timing

You may discover that different models cook at different temperatures. Therefore, you should check the texture of the ingredients so that you don't burn or under-cook them. And remember, my tips are not written in stone so you shouldn't take them as gospel. Feel free to adjust and experiment with details according to your preference and common sense.

Using oil sprays

It doesn't matter what brand you go with, so you can choose your favorite one. I use PAM. You can also use olive oil and put it into a small spray bottle.

BREAKFAST RECIPES

1. Sausage and Egg Breakfast Burrito

Preparation time: 5 minutes

Cooking time: 30 minutes

Servings: 6

Ingredients:

- 6 eggs
- Salt
- Pepper
- Cooking oil
- ½ cup chopped red bell pepper
- ½ cup chopped green bell pepper
- 8 ounces ground chicken sausage
- ½ cup salsa
- 6 media (8-inch) flour tortillas
- ½ cup shredded Cheddar cheese

Direction:

1. In a medium bowl, whisk the eggs. Add salt and pepper to taste.

2. Place a skillet on medium-high heat. Spray with cooking oil. Add the eggs. Scramble for 2 to 3 minutes, until the eggs are fluffy. Remove the eggs from the skillet and set aside.

3. If needed, spray the skillet with more oil. Add the chopped red and green bell peppers. Cook for 2 to 3 minutes, until the peppers are soft.

4. Add the ground sausage to the skillet. Break the sausage into smaller pieces using a spatula or spoon. Cook for 3 to 4 minutes, until the sausage is brown.

5. Add the salsa and scrambled eggs. Stir to combine. Remove the skillet from heat.

6. Spoon the mixture evenly onto the tortillas.

7. To form the burritos, fold the sides of each tortilla in toward the middle and then roll up from the bottom. You can secure each burrito with a toothpick. Or you can moisten the outside edge of the tortilla with a small amount of water. I

prefer to use a cooking brush, but you can also dab with your fingers.

8. Spray the burritos with cooking oil and place them in the air fryer. Do not stack. Cook the burritos in batches if they do not all fit in the basket. Cook for 8 minutes.

9. Open the air fryer and flip the burritos. Cook for an additional 2 minutes or until crisp.

10. If necessary, repeat steps 8 and 9 for the remaining burritos.

11. Sprinkle the Cheddar cheese over the burritos. Cool before serving.

Nutrition: Calories: 236;Total fat: 13g;Saturated fat: 5g;Cholesterol: 174mg;Sodium: 439mg;Carbohydrates: 16g;Fiber: 2g;Protein: 15g

2. Eggs in Avocado

Preparation time: 8 minutes

Cooking time: 15 minutes

Servings: 2

Ingredients:

- 1 avocado, pitted
- ¼ teaspoon turmeric
- ¼ teaspoon ground black pepper
- ¼ teaspoon salt
- 2 eggs
- 1 teaspoon butter
- ¼ teaspoon flax seeds

Directions:

1. Take a shallow bowl and add the turmeric, ground black pepper, salt, and flax seeds together. Shake gently to combine. Cut the avocado into 2 halves.

2. Crack the eggs in a separate bowl.

3. Sprinkle the eggs with the spice mixture.

4. Place the eggs in the avocado halves.

5. Put the avocado boats in the Air Fryer.

6. Set the Air Fryer to 355 F and close it.

7. Cook the dish for 15 minutes or until the eggs are cooked to preference.

8. Serve immediately.

Nutrition: calories 288 fat 26 fiber 6.9 carbs 9.4 protein 7.6

3. French Toast Sticks

Preparation time: 5 minutes

Cooking time: 15 minutes

Servings: 1

Ingredients:

- 4 slices Texas toast (or any thick bread, such as challah)

- 1 tablespoon butter

- 1 egg

- 1 teaspoon stevia

- 1 teaspoon ground cinnamon

- ¼ cup milk

- 1 teaspoon vanilla extract

- Cooking oil

Directions:

1. Cut each slice of bread into 3 pieces (for 12 sticks total).

2. Place the butter in a small, microwave-safe bowl. Microwave for 15 seconds, or until the butter has melted.

3. Remove the bowl from the microwave. Add the egg, stevia, cinnamon, milk, and vanilla extract. Whisk until fully combined.

4. Spray the air fryer basket with cooking oil.

5. Dredge each of the bread sticks in the egg mixture.

6. Place the French toast sticks in the air fryer. It is okay to stack them. Spray the French toast sticks with cooking oil. Cook for 8 minutes.

7. Open the air fryer and flip each of the French toast sticks. Cook for an additional 4 minutes, or until the French toast sticks are crisp.

8. Cool before serving.

Nutrition: Calories: 52; Total fat: 2g; Saturated fat: 1g; Cholesterol: 17mg; Sodium: 81mg; Carbohydrates: 7g; Fiber: 0g;Protein: 2g

4. Home-Fried Potatoes

Preparation time: 5 minutes

Cooking time: 25 minutes

Servings: 4

Ingredients:

- 3 large russet potatoes

- 1 tablespoon canola oil

- 1 tablespoon extra-virgin olive oil

- 1 teaspoon paprika

- Salt

- Pepper

- 1 cup chopped onion

- 1 cup chopped red bell pepper

- 1 cup chopped green bell pepper

Directions:

1. Cut the potatoes into ½-inch cubes. Place the potatoes in a large bowl of cold water and allow them to soak for at least 30 minutes, preferably an hour.

2. Drain the potatoes and dry thoroughly with paper towels. Return them to the empty bowl.

3. Add the canola and olive oils, paprika, and salt and pepper to taste. Toss to fully coat the potatoes.

4. Transfer the potatoes to the air fryer. Cook for 20 minutes, shaking the air fryer basket every 5 minutes (a total of 4 times).

5. Add the onion and red and green bell peppers to the air fryer basket. Cook for an additional 3 to 4 minutes, or until the potatoes are cooked through and the peppers are soft.

6. Cool before serving.

Nutrition: Calories: 279; Total fat: 8g; Saturated fat: 1g; Cholesterol: 0mg; Sodium: 58mg; Carbohydrates: 50g; Fiber: 8g; Protein: 6g

5. <u>Homemade Cherry Breakfast Tarts</u>

Preparation time: 15 minutes

Cooking time: 20 minutes

Servings: 6

Ingredients:

For the tarts:

- 2 refrigerated piecrusts

- 1/3 cup cherry preserves

- 1 teaspoon cornstarch

- Cooking oil

For the frosting:

- ½ cup vanilla yogurt

- 1-ounce cream cheese

- 1 teaspoon stevia

- Rainbow sprinkles

Directions:

1. To make the tarts:

2. Place the piecrusts on a flat surface. Using a knife or pizza cutter, cut each piecrust into 3 rectangles, for 6 total. (I discard the unused dough left from slicing the edges.)

3. In a small bowl, combine the preserves and cornstarch. Mix well.

4. Scoop 1 tablespoon of the preserves mixture onto the top half of each piece of piecrust.

5. Fold the bottom of each piece up to close the tart. Using the back of a fork, press along the edges of each tart to seal.

6. Spray the breakfast tarts with cooking oil and place them in the air fryer. I do not recommend stacking the breakfast tarts. They will stick together if stacked. You may need to prepare them in two batches. Cook for 10 minutes.

7. Allow the breakfast tarts to cool fully before removing from the air fryer.

8. If necessary, repeat steps 5 and 6 for the remaining breakfast tarts.

9. To make the frosting:

10. In a small bowl, combine the yogurt, cream cheese, and stevia. Mix well.

11. Spread the breakfast tarts with frosting and top with sprinkles, and serve.

Nutrition: Calories: 119; Total fat: 4g; Saturated fat: 2g; Cholesterol: 8mg; Sodium: 81mg; Carbohydrates: 19g; Fiber: 0g; Protein: 2g

MAIN DISH

6. Roasted Salmon with Lemon and Rosemary

Preparation time: 10 minutes

Cooking time: 10 minutes

Servings: 4

Ingredients:

- 4 salmon steak

- 2 tablespoons. unsalted butter

- 2 tablespoons. lemon juice

- 1 teaspoon. garlic, minced

- 2 tablespoons. freshly chopped rosemary

- Himalayan salt

- freshly ground black pepper

Directions:

1. In a dish mix garlic, butter, rosemary, and lemon juice; add the salmon steaks and rub with a mixture. Cover and let it sit inside the refrigerator for 30 minutes.

2. Preheat your Air Fryer to 390°F.

3. Place the marinated salmon steaks in cooking basket and cook for about 8-10 minutes.

4. Transfer into a serving dish. Garnish with fresh rosemary leaves.

5. Serve and enjoy!

Nutrition: Calories: 209 Fat: 12.1 g Carbs: 2.3 g Protein: 22.4 g

7. <u>Air Fried Meatballs with Parsley</u>

Preparation time: 5 minutes

Cooking time: 10 minutes

Servings: 5

Ingredients:

- 1 chopped onion

- 1 teaspoon. minced garlic

- 1 lb. lean ground beef

- ¼ c. chopped parsley leaves

- ½ teaspoon. ground coriander seeds

- ¼ teaspoon. ground fennel seeds

- 1 egg

- 2 teaspoons. Worcestershire sauce

- ½ c. breadcrumbs

- sea salt

- ground black pepper

Directions:

1. In a mixing bowl, mix all ingredients.

2. Take about 2 tablespoons of beef mixture and form into small balls.

3. Preheat your Air Fryer to 390°F.

4. Place meatballs in the Air Fryer basket and cook until browned for 10 minutes.

5. Set into a serving bowl and spread with parsley.

6. Enjoy!

Nutrition: Calories: 233 Fat: 7.2g Carbs: 10.3g Protein: 30.3g

8. Succulent Flank Steak

Preparation time: 10 minutes

Cooking time: 15 minutes

Servings: 4

Ingredients:

- 4 flank steak

- ¼ c. olive oil

- ¼ c. red wine vinegar

- 1 tablespoon. light soy sauce

- 1 Tablespoon. Worcestershire sauce

- 1 Tablespoon. Dijon mustard

- 1 teaspoon. garlic, minced

- Salt and ground black pepper

Directions:

1. In a non-reactive bowl, combine together olive oil, red wine vinegar, light soy sauce, Worcestershire sauce, Dijon mustard, and garlic. Add the steaks and mix to coat well. Cover and let it sit for 30 minutes inside the refrigerator.

2. Preheat Air Fryer to 360°F.

3. Place marinated steaks inside the Air Fryer cooking basket and cook for about 6-7 minutes (medium-rare) or 8-10 minutes (well-done).

4. Transfer into a serving dish.

5. Serve and enjoy!

Nutrition: Calories: 280 Fat: 14.2g Carbs: 1.5g Protein: 34.1 g

9. Chili Roasted Eggplant Soba

Preparation time: 15 minutes

Cooking time: 10 minutes

Servings: 4

Ingredients:

- 200g eggplants

- Kosher salt

- Ground black pepper

- Noodles:

- 8 oz. soba noodles

- 1 c. sliced button mushrooms

- 2 tablespoons. peanut oil

- 2 tablespoons. light soy sauce

- 1 Tablespoon. rice vinegar

- 2 tablespoons. chopped cilantro

- 2 chopped red chili pepper

- 1 teaspoon. sesame oil

Directions:

1. In a mixing bowl, mix together ingredients for the marinade.

2. Wash eggplants and then slice into ¼-inch thick cuts. Season with salt and pepper, to taste.

3. Preheat your Air Fryer to 390°F.

4. Place eggplants in the Air Fryer cooking basket. Cook for 10 minutes.

5. Meanwhile, cook the soba noodles according to packaging directions. Drain the noodles.

6. In a large mixing bowl, combine the peanut oil, soy sauce, rice vinegar, cilantro, chili, and sesame oil. Mix well.

7. Add the cooked soba noodles, mushrooms, and roasted eggplants; toss to coat.

8. Transfer mixture into the Air Fryer cooking basket. Cook for another 5 minutes.

9. Serve and enjoy!

Nutrition: Calories: 318 Fat: 8.2g Carbs: 54g Protein: 11.3g

10. Quinoa and Spinach Cakes

Preparation time: 10 minutes

Cooking time: 10 minutes

Servings: 10

Ingredients:

- 2 c. cooked quinoa

- 1 c. chopped baby spinach

- 1 egg

- 2 tablespoons. minced parsley

- 1 teaspoon. minced garlic

- 1 carrot, peeled and shredded

- 1 chopped onion

- ¼ c. skim milk

- ¼ c. parmesan cheese, grated

- 1 c. breadcrumbs

- sea salt

- Ground black pepper

Directions:

1. In a mixing bowl, mix all ingredients. Season with salt and pepper to taste. Preheat your Air Fryer to 390°F.

2. Scoop 1/4 cup of quinoa and spinach mixture and place in the Air Fryer cooking basket. Cook in batches until browned for about 8 minutes.

3. Serve and enjoy!

Nutrition: Calories: 188 Fat: 4.4 g Carbs: 31.2g Protein: 8.1g

11. <u>Air Fried Cajun Shrimp</u>

Preparation time: 5 minutes

Cooking time: 8 minutes

Servings: 5

Ingredients:

- 1 lb. fresh shrimp

- 2 tablespoons. olive oil

- 1 teaspoon. Spanish paprika

- ½ teaspoon. garlic powder

- ½ teaspoon. ground cumin

- ¼ teaspoon. oregano

- ¼ teaspoon. thyme

- ¼ teaspoon. ground black pepper

- ¼ teaspoon. sea salt

Directions:

1. In a bowl, mix all spice ingredients.

2. Add the shrimps and drizzle with olive oil. Toss to coat well. Cover and place inside the refrigerator to 30 minutes.

3. Preheat your Air Fryer to 390°F.

4. Transfer the shrimps into your Air Fryer cooking basket and cook for about 5-7 minutes.

5. Serve immediately and enjoy!

Nutrition: Calories: 156 Fat: 7.2 g Carbs: 3.8 g Protein: 22.3 g

SIDE DISHES

12. Parmesan Sweet Potato Casserole

Preparation time: 15 minutes

Cooking time: 35 minutes

Servings: 2

Ingredients:

- 2 sweet potatoes, peeled

- ½ yellow onion, sliced

- ½ cup cream

- ¼ cup spinach

- 2 oz. Parmesan cheese, shredded

- ½ teaspoon salt

- 1 tomato

- 1 teaspoon olive oil

Directions:

1. Chop the sweet potatoes.

2. Chop the tomato.

3. Chop the spinach.

4. Spray the air fryer tray with the olive oil.

5. Then place on the layer of the chopped sweet potato.

6. Add the layer of the sliced onion.

7. After this, sprinkle the sliced onion with the chopped spinach and tomatoes.

8. Sprinkle the casserole with the salt and shredded cheese.

9. Pour cream.

10. Preheat the air fryer to 390 F.

11. Cover the air fryer tray with the foil.

12. Cook the casserole for 35 minutes.

13. When the casserole is cooked – serve it.

14. Enjoy!

Nutrition: calories 93, fat 1.8, fiber 3.4, carbs 20.3, protein 1.8

13. <u>Spicy Zucchini Slices</u>

Preparation time: 10 minutes

Cooking time: 6 minutes

Servings: 2

Ingredients:

- 1 teaspoon cornstarch

- 1 zucchini

- ½ teaspoon chili flakes

- 1 tablespoon flour

- 1 egg

- ¼ teaspoon salt

Directions:

1. Slice the zucchini and sprinkle with the chili flakes and salt.

2. Crack the egg into the bowl and whisk it.

3. Dip the zucchini slices in the whisked egg.

4. Combine together cornstarch with the flour. Stir it.

5. Coat the zucchini slices with the cornstarch mixture.

6. Preheat the air fryer to 400 F.

7. Place the zucchini slices in the air fryer tray.

8. Cook the zucchini slices for 4 minutes.

9. After this, flip the slices to another side and cook for 2 minutes more.

10. Serve the zucchini slices hot.

11. Enjoy!

Nutrition: calories 67, fat 2.4, fiber 1.2, carbs 7.7, protein 4.4

14. Cheddar Potato Gratin

Preparation time: 15 minutes

Cooking time: 20 minutes

Servings: 2

Ingredients:

- 2 potatoes

- 1/3 cup half and half

- 1 tablespoon oatmeal flour

- ¼ teaspoon ground black pepper

- 1 egg

- 2 oz. Cheddar cheese

Directions:

1. Wash the potatoes and slice them into thin pieces.

2. Preheat the air fryer to 365 F.

3. Put the potato slices in the air fryer and cook them for 10 minutes.

4. Meanwhile, combine the half and half, oatmeal flour, and ground black pepper.

5. Crack the egg into the liquid and whisk it carefully.

6. Shred Cheddar cheese.

7. When the potato is cooked – take 2 ramekins and place the potatoes on them.

8. Pour the half and half mixture.

9. Sprinkle the gratin with shredded Cheddar cheese.

10. Cook the gratin for 10 minutes at 360 F.

11. Serve the meal immediately.

12. Enjoy!

Nutrition: calories 353, fat 16.6, fiber 5.4, carbs 37.2, protein 15

15. <u>Salty Lemon Artichokes</u>

Preparation time: 15 minutes

Cooking time: 45 minutes

Servings: 2

Ingredients:

- 1 lemon

- 2 artichokes

- 1 teaspoon kosher salt

- 1 garlic head

- 2 teaspoons olive oil

Directions:

1. Cut off the edges of the artichokes.

2. Cut the lemon into the halves.

3. Peel the garlic head and chop the garlic cloves roughly.

4. Then place the chopped garlic in the artichokes.

5. Sprinkle the artichokes with the olive oil and kosher salt.

6. Then squeeze the lemon juice into the artichokes.

7. Wrap the artichokes in the foil.

8. Preheat the air fryer to 330 F.

9. Place the wrapped artichokes in the air fryer and cook for 45 minutes.

10. When the artichokes are cooked – discard the foil and serve.

11. Enjoy!

Nutrition: calories 133, fat 5, fiber 9.7, carbs 21.7, protein 6

SEAFOOD RECIPES

16. Delicious Crab Cakes

Preparation Time: 10 minutes

Cooking Time: 10 minutes

Servings: 4

Ingredients:

- 8 oz. crab meat

- 2 tablespoon. butter, melted

- 2 teaspoon Dijon mustard

- tablespoon. mayonnaise

- 1 egg, lightly beaten

- 1/2 teaspoon old bay seasoning

- 1 green onion, sliced

- 2 tablespoon. parsley, chopped

- 1/4 cup almond flour

- 1/4 teaspoon pepper

- 1/2 teaspoon salt

Directions:

1. Add all ingredients except butter in a mixing bowl and mix until well combined.

2. Make four equal shapes of patties from mixture and place on parchment lined plate.

3. Place plate in the fridge for 30 minutes.

4. Spray air fryer basket with cooking spray.

5. Brush melted butter on both sides of crab patties.

6. Place crab patties in air fryer basket and cook for 10 minutes at 350 F.

7. Turn patties halfway through.

8. Serve and enjoy.

Nutrition: Calories 136 Fat 12.6 g Carbohydrates 4.1 g Sugar 0.5 g Protein 10.3 g Cholesterol 88 mg

17. <u>Tuna Patties</u>

Preparation Time: 10 minutes

Cooking Time: 10 minutes

Servings: 2

Ingredients:

- 2 cans tuna
- 1/2 lemon juice
- 1/2 teaspoon onion powder
- 1 teaspoon garlic powder
- 1/2 teaspoon dried dill
- 1 1/2 tablespoon. mayonnaise
- 1 1/2 tablespoon. almond flour
- 1/4 teaspoon pepper
- 1/4 teaspoon salt

Directions:

1. Preheat the air fryer to 400 F. Add all ingredients in a mixing bowl and mix until well combined.

2. Spray air fryer basket with cooking spray.

3. Make four patties from mixture and place in the air fryer basket.

4. Cook patties for 10 minutes at 400 F if you want crispier patties then cook for 3 minutes more.

5. Serve and enjoy.

Nutrition: Calories 414 Fat 20.6 g Carbohydrates 5.6 g Sugar 1.3 g Protein 48.8 g Cholesterol 58 mg

18. <u>Crispy Fish Sticks</u>

Preparation Time: 10 minutes

Cooking Time: 10 minutes

Servings: 4

Ingredients:

- 1 lb. white fish, cut into pieces

- 3/4 teaspoon Cajun seasoning

- 1 1/2 cups pork rind, crushed

- 2 tablespoon. water

- 2 tablespoon. Dijon mustard

- 1/4 cup mayonnaise

- Pepper

- Salt

Directions:

1. Spray air fryer basket with cooking spray. In a small bowl, whisk together mayonnaise, water, and mustard.

2. In a shallow bowl, mix together pork rind, pepper, Cajun seasoning, and salt.

3. Dip fish pieces in mayo mixture and coat with pork rind mixture and place in the air fryer basket.

4. Cook at 400 F for 5 minutes. Turn fish sticks to another side and cook for 5 minutes more.

5. Serve and enjoy.

Nutrition: Calories 397 Fat 36.4 g Carbohydrates 4 g Sugar 1 g Protein 14.7 g Cholesterol 4 mg

19. Flavorful Parmesan Shrimp

Preparation Time: 10 minutes

Cooking Time: 10 minutes

Servings: 6

Ingredients:

- 2 lbs. cooked shrimp, peeled and deveined

- 2 tablespoon. olive oil

- 1/2 teaspoon onion powder

- 1 teaspoon basil

- 1/2 teaspoon oregano

- 2/3 cup parmesan cheese, grated

- 3 garlic cloves, minced

- 1/4 teaspoon pepper

Directions:

1. In a large mixing bowl, combine together garlic, oil, onion powder, oregano, pepper, and cheese.

2. Add shrimp in a bowl and toss until well coated.

3. Spray air fryer basket with cooking spray.

4. Add shrimp into the air fryer basket and cook at 350 F for 8-10 minutes.

5. Serve and enjoy.

Nutrition: Calories 233 Fat 7.9 g Carbohydrates 3.2 g Sugar 0.1 g Protein 35.6 g Cholesterol 32 m

POULTRY RECIPES

20. Korean Chicken Wings

Preparation time: 10 minutes

Cooking time: 25 minutes

Servings: 4

Ingredients:

Wings:

- 1 teaspoon. pepper

- 1 teaspoon. salt

- 2 pounds' chicken wings

Sauce:

- 2 packets Splenda

- 1 tablespoon. minced garlic

- 1 tablespoon. minced ginger

- 1 tablespoon. sesame oil

- 1 teaspoon. agave nectar

- 1 tablespoon. mayo

- 2 tablespoon. gochujang

Finishing:

- ¼ C. chopped green onions
- 2 teaspoon. sesame seeds

Directions:

1. Ensure air fryer is preheated to 400 degrees.
2. Line a small pan with foil and place a rack onto the pan, then place into air fryer.
3. Season wings with pepper and salt and place onto the rack.
4. Air fry 20 minutes, turning at 10 minutes.
5. As chicken air fries, mix together all the sauce components.
6. Once a thermometer says that the chicken has reached 160 degrees, take out wings and place into a bowl.
7. Pour half of the sauce mixture over wings, tossing well to coat.
8. Put coated wings back into air fryer for 5 minutes or till they reach 165 degrees.
9. Remove and sprinkle with green onions and sesame seeds. Dip into extra sauce.

Nutrition: Calories: 356 Fat: 26g Protein: 23g Sugar: 2g

21. <u>Buffalo Chicken Wings</u>

Preparation time: 15 minutes

Cooking time: 30 minutes

Servings: 8

Ingredients:

- 1 teaspoon. salt

- 1-2 tablespoon. brown sugar

- 1 tablespoon. Worcestershire sauce

- ½ C. vegan butter

- ½ C. cayenne pepper sauce

- 4 pounds' chicken wings

Directions:

1. Whisk salt, brown sugar, Worcestershire sauce, butter, and hot sauce together and set to the side.

2. Dry wings and add to air fryer basket.

3. Cook 25 minutes at 380 degrees, tossing halfway through.

4. When timer sounds, shake wings and bump up the temperature to 400 degrees and cook another 5 minutes.

5. Take out wings and place into a big bowl. Add sauce and toss well.

6. Serve alongside celery sticks!

Nutrition: Calories: 402 Fat: 16g Protein: 17g Sugar: 4g

MEAT RECIPES

22. Seasoned Rib-Eye Steak

Preparation Time: 10 minutes

Cooking Time: 14 minutes

Servings: 3

Ingredients:

- 2 (8-ounce) rib-eye steaks

- 2 tablespoons olive oil

- 1 tablespoon steak seasoning

- Salt and ground black pepper, as required

Directions:

1. Coat the steaks with oil and then, sprinkle with seasoning, salt and black pepper evenly. Arrange the steaks onto the steak tray. Select "Steak" of Kalorik Digital Air Fryer Oven and then adjust the temperature to 400 degrees F. Set the timer for 14 minutes and press "Start/Stop" to begin cooking. When the unit beeps to show that it is preheated, insert the steak tray in the Kalorik Oven. When cooking time

is complete, remove the steaks from Kalorik oven and place onto a cutting board for about 5 minutes.

2. Cut each steak into desired size slices and serve.

Nutrition: Calories 495 Total Fat 42.8 g Saturated Fat 14.7 g Cholesterol 100 mg Sodium 137 mg Total Carbs 0 g Fiber 0 g Sugar 0 g Protein 26.8 g

23. Spiced Sirloin Steak

Preparation Time: 10 minutes

Cooking Time: 12 minutes

Servings: 2

Ingredients:

- 2 (7-ounce) top sirloin steaks

- ½ teaspoon dried rosemary, crushed

- ½ teaspoon ground cumin

- ½ teaspoon cayenne pepper

- Salt and ground black pepper, as required

Directions:

1. In a small bowl, mix together rosemary, spices, salt and black pepper. Season each steak with spice mixture generously.

2. Arrange the steaks onto the greased steak tray. Select "Air Fry" of Kalorik Digital Air Fryer Oven and then adjust the temperature to 400 degrees F. Set the timer for 12 minutes and press "Start/Stop" to begin cooking.

3. When the unit beeps to show that it is preheated, insert the steak tray in the Kalorik Oven.

4. Flip the steaks once halfway through.

5. When cooking time is complete, remove the steaks from Kalorik oven and place onto a platter for about 5 minutes before serving.

Nutrition: Calories 373 Total Fat 12.6 g Saturated Fat 4.7 g Cholesterol 177 mg Sodium 209 mg Total Carbs 0.7 g Fiber 0.3 g Sugar 0.1 g Protein 60.4 g

24. Herbed Flank Steak

Preparation Time: 10 minutes

Cooking Time: 12 minutes

Servings: 6

Ingredients:

- 2 tablespoons fresh lemon juice

- 2 tablespoons olive oil

- 1 teaspoon fresh rosemary, minced

- 1 teaspoon fresh thyme, minced

- 1 teaspoon fresh oregano, minced

- 1 teaspoon garlic powder

- Salt and ground black pepper, as required

- 1 (2-pound) flank steak

Directions:

1. In a large bowl, mix together the lemon juice, oil, herbs, garlic powder, salt and black pepper.

2. Add the steak and coat with mixture generously.

3. Cover the bowl and place in the refrigerator for at least 1 hour.

4. Arrange the steak onto the greased steak tray.

5. Select "Broil" of Kalorik Digital Air Fryer Oven and then set the timer for 12 minutes.

6. Press "Start/Stop" to begin cooking.

7. Flip the steak once halfway through.

8. When the unit beeps to show that it is preheated, insert the steak tray in the Kalorik Oven.

9. When cooking time is complete, remove the steak from Kalorik oven and place onto a cutting board for about 5 minutes.

10. Cut the steak into desired size slices and serve.

Nutrition: Calories 338 Total Fat 17.4 g Saturated Fat 6 g Cholesterol 83 mg Sodium 113 mg Total Carbs 0.9 g Fiber 0.3 g Sugar 0.2 g Protein 42.2 g

25. Seasoned Beef Tenderloin

Preparation Time: 10 minutes

Cooking Time: 50 minutes

Servings: 10

Ingredients:

- 1 (3½-pound) beef tenderloin, trimmed

- 2 tablespoons olive oil

- 3 tablespoons Montreal steak seasoning

Directions:

1. With kitchen twine, tie the tenderloin.

2. Rub the tenderloin with oil and season with seasoning.

3. Place the tenderloin into the greased baking pan.

4. Select "Roast" of Kalorik Digital Air Fryer Oven and then adjust the temperature to 400 degrees F.

5. Set the timer for 50 minutes and press "Start/Stop" to begin cooking.

6. When the unit beeps to show that it is preheated, insert the baking pan in the Kalorik Oven.

7. When cooking time is complete, remove the tenderloin from Kalorik Oven and place onto a cutting board for about 10 minutes before slicing.

8. With a sharp knife, cut the tenderloin into desired sized slices and serve.

Nutrition: Calories 357 Total Fat 17.3 g Saturated Fat 5.9 g Cholesterol 146 mg Sodium 766 mg Total Carbs 0 g Fiber 0 g Sugar 0 g Protein 46 g

26. Simple Beef Sirloin Roast

Preparation Time: 10 minutes

Cooking Time: 50 minutes

Servings: 8

Ingredients:

- 2½ pounds sirloin roast

- Salt and ground black pepper, as required

Directions:

1. Rub the roast with salt and black pepper generously.

2. Place the sirloin roast into the greased baking pan.

3. Select "Roast" of Kalorik Digital Air Fryer Oven and then adjust the temperature to 350 degrees F.

4. Set the timer for 50 minutes and press "Start/Stop" to begin cooking.

5. When the unit beeps to show that it is preheated, insert the baking pan in the Kalorik Oven.

6. When cooking time is complete, remove the sirloin roast from Kalorik Oven and place onto a cutting board for about 10 minutes before slicing.

7. With a sharp knife, cut the beef roast into desired sized slices and serve.

Nutrition: Calories 301 Total Fat 20.1 g Saturated Fat 8.8 g Cholesterol 75 mg Sodium 95 mg Total Carbs 0 g Fiber 0 g Sugar 0 g Protein 28.9 g

VEGETABLE RECIPES

27. Baby Corn in Chili-Turmeric Spice

Preparation time: 5 minutes

Cooking time: 8 minutes

Servings: 5

Ingredients:

- ¼ cup water

- ¼ teaspoon baking soda

- ¼ teaspoon salt

- ¼ teaspoon turmeric powder

- ½ teaspoon curry powder

- ½ teaspoon red chili powder

- 1 cup chickpea flour or besan

- 10 pieces' baby corn, blanched

Directions:

1. Preheat the air fryer to 4000F.

2. Line the air fryer basket with aluminum foil and brush with oil.

3. In a mixing bowl, mix all ingredients except for the corn.

4. Whisk until well combined.

5. Dip the corn in the batter and place inside the air fryer. Cook for 8 minutes until golden brown.

Nutrition: Calories: 89; Carbohydrates: 14.35g; Protein: 4.75g; Fat: 1.54g

28. Baked Cheesy Eggplant with Marinara

Preparation time: 20 minutes

Cooking time: 45 minutes

Servings: 3

Ingredients:

- 1 clove garlic, sliced

- 1 large eggplants

- 1 tablespoon olive oil

- 1 tablespoon olive oil

- 1/2 pinch salt, or as needed

- 1/4 cup and 2 tablespoons dry bread crumbs

- 1/4 cup and 2 tablespoons ricotta cheese

- 1/4 cup grated Parmesan cheese

- 1/4 cup grated Parmesan cheese

- 1/4 cup water, plus more as needed

- 1/4 teaspoon red pepper flakes

- 1-1/2 cups prepared marinara sauce

- 1-1/2 teaspoons olive oil

- 2 tablespoons shredded pepper jack cheese

- salt and freshly ground black pepper to taste

Directions:

1. Cut eggplant crosswise in 5 pieces. Peel and chop two pieces into ½-inch cubes.

2. Lightly grease baking pan of air fryer with 1 tablespoon. olive oil. For 5 minutes, heat oil at 390oF. Add half eggplant strips and cook for 2 minutes per side. Transfer to a plate.

3. Add 1 ½ teaspoon olive oil and add garlic. Cook for a minute. Add chopped eggplants. Season with pepper flakes and salt.

4. Cook for 4 minutes. Lower heat to 330oF and continue cooking eggplants until soft, around 8 minutes more.

5. Stir in water and marinara sauce. Cook for 7 minutes until heated through. Stirring every now and then. Transfer to a bowl.

6. In a bowl, whisk well pepper, salt, pepper jack cheese, Parmesan cheese, and ricotta. Evenly spread cheeses over eggplant strips and then fold in half.

7. Lay folded eggplant in baking pan. Pour marinara sauce on top.

8. In a small bowl whisk well olive oil, and bread crumbs. Sprinkle all over sauce.

9. Cook for 15 minutes at 390oF until tops are lightly browned.

10. Serve and enjoy.

Nutrition: Calories: 405; Carbs: 41.1g; Protein: 12.7g; Fat: 21.4g

29. Baked Polenta with Chili-Cheese

Preparation time: minutes

Cooking time: 10 minutes

Servings: 3

Ingredients:

- 1 commercial polenta roll, sliced

- 1 cup cheddar cheese sauce

- 1 tablespoon chili powder

Directions:

1. Place the baking dish accessory in the air fryer.

2. Arrange the polenta slices in the baking dish.

3. Add the chili powder and cheddar cheese sauce.

4. Close the air fryer and cook for 10 minutes at 3900F.

Nutrition: Calories: 206; Carbs: 25.3g; Protein: 3.2g; Fat: 4.2g

30. Baked Portobello, Pasta 'n Cheese

Preparation time: 10 minutes

Cooking time: 30 minutes

Servings: 4

Ingredients:

- 1 cup milk

- 1 cup shredded mozzarella cheese

- 1 large clove garlic, minced

- 1 tablespoon vegetable oil

- 1/4 cup margarine

- 1/4 teaspoon dried basil

- 1/4-pound Portobello mushrooms, thinly sliced

- 2 tablespoons all-purpose flour

- 2 tablespoons soy sauce

- 4-ounce penne pasta, cooked according to manufacturer's Directions for Cooking

- 5-ounce frozen chopped spinach, thawed

Directions:

1. Lightly grease baking pan of air fryer with oil. For 2 minutes, heat on 360oF. Add mushrooms and cook for a minute. Transfer to a plate.

2. In same pan, melt margarine for a minute. Stir in basil, garlic, and flour. Cook for 3 minutes. Stir and cook for another 2 minutes.

3. Stir in half of milk slowly while whisking continuously. Cook for another 2 minutes. Mix well. Cook for another 2 minutes. Stir in remaining milk and cook for another 3 minutes.

4. Add cheese and mix well.

5. Stir in soy sauce, spinach, mushrooms, and pasta. Mix well. Top with remaining cheese.

6. Cook for 15 minutes at 390oF until tops are lightly browned.

Nutrition: Calories: 482; Carbs: 32.1g; Protein: 16.0g; Fat: 32.1g

31. Baked Potato Topped with Cream cheese 'n Olives

Preparation time: 15 minutes

Cooking time: 40 minutes

Servings: 1

Ingredients:

- ¼ teaspoon onion powder

- 1 medium russet potato, scrubbed and peeled

- 1 tablespoon chives, chopped

- 1 tablespoon Kalamata olives

- 1 teaspoon olive oil

- 1/8 teaspoon salt

- a dollop of vegan butter

- a dollop of vegan cream cheese

Directions:

1. Place inside the air fryer basket and cook for 40 minutes. Be sure to turn the potatoes once halfway.

2. Place the potatoes in a mixing bowl and pour in olive oil, onion powder, salt, and vegan butter.

3. Preheat the air fryer to 4000F.

4. Serve the potatoes with vegan cream cheese, Kalamata olives, chives, and other vegan toppings that you want.

Nutrition: Calories :504; Carbohydrates: 68.34g; Protein: 9.31g; Fat: 21.53g

32. Baked Zucchini Recipe from Mexico

Preparation time: 10 minutes

Cooking time: 30 minutes

Servings: 4

Ingredients:

- 1 tablespoon olive oil

- 1-1/2 pounds' zucchini, cubed

- 1/2 cup chopped onion

- 1/2 teaspoon garlic salt

- 1/2 teaspoon paprika

- 1/2 teaspoon dried oregano

- 1/2 teaspoon cayenne pepper, or to taste

- 1/2 cup cooked long-grain rice

- 1/2 cup cooked pinto beans

- 1-1/4 cups salsa

- 3/4 cup shredded Cheddar cheese

Directions:

1. Lightly grease baking pan of air fryer with olive oil. Add onions and zucchini and for 10 minutes, cook on 360oF. Halfway through cooking time, stir.

2. Season with cayenne, oregano, paprika, and garlic salt. Mix well.

3. Stir in salsa, beans, and rice. Cook for 5 minutes.

4. Stir in cheddar cheese and mix well.

5. Cover pan with foil.

6. Cook for 15 minutes at 390oF until bubbly.

7. Serve and enjoy.

Nutrition: Calories: 263; Carbs: 24.6g; Protein: 12.5g; Fat: 12.7g

33. Banana Pepper Stuffed with Tofu 'n Spices

Preparation time: 5 minutes

Cooking time: 10 minutes

Servings: 8

Ingredients:

- ½ teaspoon red chili powder

- ½ teaspoon turmeric powder

- 1 onion, finely chopped

- 1 package firm tofu, crumbled

- 1 teaspoon coriander powder

- 3 tablespoons coconut oil

- 8 banana peppers, top end sliced and seeded

- Salt to taste

Directions:

1. Preheat the air fryer for 5 minutes.

2. In a mixing bowl, combine the tofu, onion, coconut oil, turmeric powder, red chili powder, coriander power, and salt. Mix until well-combined.

3. Scoop the tofu mixture into the hollows of the banana peppers.

4. Place the stuffed peppers in the air fryer.

5. Close and cook for 10 minutes at 3250F.

Nutrition: Calories: 72; Carbohydrates: 4.1g; Protein: 1.2g; Fat: 5.6g

34. Bell Pepper-Corn Wrapped in Tortilla

Preparation time: 5 minutes

Cooking time: 15 minutes

Servings: 4

Ingredients:

- 1 small red bell pepper, chopped

- 1 small yellow onion, diced

- 1 tablespoon water

- 2 cobs grilled corn kernels

- 4 large tortillas

- 4 pieces' commercial vegan nuggets, chopped

- mixed greens for garnish

Directions:

1. Preheat the air fryer to 4000F.

2. In a skillet heated over medium heat, water sauté the vegan nuggets together with the onions, bell peppers, and corn kernels. Set aside.

3. Place filling inside the corn tortillas.

4. Fold the tortillas and place inside the air fryer and cook for 15 minutes until the tortilla wraps are crispy.

5. Serve with mix greens on top.

Nutrition: Calories: 548; Carbohydrates: 43.54g; Protein: 46.73g; Fat: 20.76g

35. Black Bean Burger with Garlic-Chipotle

Preparation time: 10 minutes

Cooking time: 20 minutes

Servings: 3

Ingredients:

- ½ cup corn kernels

- ½ teaspoon chipotle powder

- ½ teaspoon garlic powder

- ¾ cup salsa

- 1 ¼ teaspoon chili powder

- 1 ½ cup rolled oats

- 1 can black beans, rinsed and drained

- 1 tablespoon soy sauce

Directions:

1. In a mixing bowl, combine all **Ingredients:** and mix using your hands.

2. Form small patties using your hands and set aside.

3. Brush patties with oil if desired.

4. Place the grill pan in the air fryer and place the patties on the grill pan accessory.

5. Close the lid and cook for 20 minutes on each side at 3300F.

Nutrition: Calories: 395; Carbs: 52.2g; Protein: 24.3g; Fat: 5.8g

36. Brown Rice, Spinach 'n Tofu Frittata

Preparation time: 20 minutes

Cooking time: 55 minutes

Servings: 4

Ingredients:

- ½ cup baby spinach, chopped

- ½ cup kale, chopped

- ½ onion, chopped

- ½ teaspoon turmeric

- 1 ¾ cups brown rice, cooked

- 1 flax egg (1 tablespoon flaxseed meal + 3 tablespoon cold water)

- 1 package firm tofu

- 1 tablespoon olive oil

- 1 yellow pepper, chopped

- 2 tablespoons soy sauce

- 2 teaspoons arrowroot powder

- 2 teaspoons Dijon mustard

- 2/3 cup almond milk

- 3 big mushrooms, chopped

- 3 tablespoons nutritional yeast

- 4 cloves garlic, crushed

- 4 spring onions, chopped

- a handful of basil leaves, chopped

Directions:

1. Preheat the air fryer to 3750F. Grease a pan that will fit inside the air fryer.

2. Prepare the frittata crust by mixing the brown rice and flax egg. Press the rice onto the baking dish until you form a crust. Brush with a little oil and cook for 10 minutes.

3. Meanwhile, heat olive oil in a skillet over medium flame and sauté the garlic and onions for 2 minutes.

4. Add the pepper and mushroom and continue stirring for 3 minutes.

5. Stir in the kale, spinach, spring onions, and basil. Remove from the pan and set aside.

6. In a food processor, pulse together the tofu, mustard, turmeric, soy sauce, nutritional yeast, vegan milk and

arrowroot powder. Pour in a mixing bowl and stir in the sautéed vegetables.

7. Pour the vegan frittata mixture over the rice crust and cook in the air fryer for 40 minutes.

Nutrition: Calories: 226; Carbohydrates: 30.44g; Protein: 10.69g; Fat: 8.05g

FAST FOOD

37. Hot Dogs

Preparation time: 5 minutes

Cooking time: 12 minutes

Servings: 2

Ingredients:

- 2 hot dogs

- 2 hot dog buns

- 2 tablespoon. of grated cheese, optional

Directions:

1. Ensure that your air fryer is preheated at 390 F for about 4 minutes.

2. Cook the two hot dogs in the air fryer for about 5 minutes, and remove.

3. Transfer the hot dog into a bun, and you may add cheese.

4. Return the dressed hot dog into the air fryer, and allow to cook for an extra 2 minutes.

Nutrition: calories 345, fat 8, fiber 22, carbs 14, protein 20

SALAD RECIPES

38. Brussel Sprout Salad

Preparation time: 20 minutes

Cooking Time: 15 minutes

Servings: 4

Ingredients:

For Salad:

- 1 pound fresh medium Brussels sprouts, trimmed and halved vertically

- 3 teaspoons olive oil

- Salt and ground black pepper, as required

- 2 apples, cored and chopped

- 1 red onion, sliced

- 4 cups lettuce, torn

For Dressing:

- 2 tablespoons extra-virgin olive oil

- 2 tablespoons fresh lemon juice

- 1 tablespoon apple cider vinegar

- 1 tablespoon honey

- 1 teaspoon Dijon mustard

- Salt and ground black pepper, as required

Directions:

1. Set the temperature of air fryer to 360 degrees F.

2. For Brussels sprout: in a bowl, add the Brussels sprout, oil, salt, and black pepper and toss to coat well.

3. Spread the Brussels sprouts onto a large baking sheet.

4. Arrange the baking sheet into air fryer basket and air fryer for about 15 minutes, flipping once halfway through.

5. Remove from air fryer and transfer the Brussel sprouts onto a plate. Set aside to cool slightly.

6. In a serving bowl, mix together the Brussel sprouts, apples, onion, and lettuce.

7. For dressing: in a bowl, add all the ingredients and beat until well combined.

8. Add the dressing and gently, stir to combine.

9. Serve immediately.

Nutrition: Calories: 235 Carbohydrate: 34.5g Protein: 4.9g Fat: 11.3g Sugar: 20.3g Sodium: 88mg

SNACK & APPETIZERS RECIPES

39. Eggplant Mix

Preparation time: 10 minutes

Cooking time: 20 minutes

Servings: 4

Ingredients:

- Eggplant (1 lb., cubed)

- Cumin (0.5 teaspoon, ground)

- Chili powder (0.5 teaspoon)

- Olive oil (2 Tablespoon.)

- Pepper and salt

- Red onion (1, chopped)

- Cherry tomatoes (1 c., halved)

Directions:

1. Turn on the air fryer and heat it to 350 degrees with some oil.

2. Add all of the ingredients, mixing around a little bit, before closing the lid.

3. After 20 minutes of cooking, allow the dish to cool down before splitting between plates and serving.

Nutrition: Calories 110 Carbs 13g Protein 9g Fat 5g

40. Garlic Kale

Preparation time: 10 minutes

Cooking time: 20 minutes

Servings: 4

Ingredients:

- Garlic cloves (4, minced)

- Pepper and salt

- Balsamic vinegar (1 Tablespoon.)

- Dried basil (1 teaspoon.)

- Ground coriander (1 teaspoon)

- Avocado oil (1 Tablespoon.)

- Kale leaves (1 lb., torn)

Directions:

1. Turn on the air fryer and let it heat up to 370 degrees.

2. Combine all the ingredients, including the oil and kale. Toss around and put the lid on top.

3. After 20 minutes, divide this mixture between the plates and serve.

Nutrition: Calories 66 Carbs 11g Protein 6g Fat 5g

41. <u>Herbed Tomatoes</u>

Preparation time: 5 minutes

Cooking time: 20 minutes

Servings: 4

Ingredients:

- Salt and pepper

- Olive oil (2 Tablespoon.)

- Italian seasoning (1 teaspoon)

- Balsamic vinegar (1 Tablespoon.)

- Oregano (1 Tablespoon., chopped)

- Chives (2 Tablespoon., chopped)

- Tomatoes (1 lb., sliced)

Directions:

1. Add the air fryer basket inside and combine the vinegar, chives, tomatoes, and the rest of the ingredients inside.

2. Turn the air fryer to 360 degrees and let this cook. After 20 minutes, take the tomatoes out and divide and serve.

Nutrition: Calories 89 Carbs 4g Fat 7g Protein 2g

42. Coriander Potatoes

Preparation time: 15 minutes

Cooking time: 25 minutes

Servings: 4

Ingredients:

- Olive oil (1 Tablespoon.)

- Chili powder (1 teaspoon)

- Garlic powder (0.5 teaspoon)

- Coriander (2 Tablespoon.)

- Tomato sauce (1 Tablespoon.)

- Pepper

- Salt

- Gold potatoes (1 lb., peeled and sliced)

Directions:

1. Turn the air fryer to 370 degrees.

2. Take out a bowl and combine potatoes with the rest of the ingredients. Add to the air fryer.

3. After 25 minutes, divide between four plates and serve.

Nutrition: Calories 210 Carbs 12g Fat 5g Protein 5g

43. Tomatoes and Green beans

Preparation time: 10 minutes

Cooking time: 20 minutes

Servings: 4

Ingredients:

- Cilantro (0.5 Tablespoon., chopped)

- Heavy cream (1 c.)

- Pepper

- Salt

- Dried basil (1 teaspoon)

- Dried oregano (1 teaspoon)

- Olive oil (2 Tablespoon.)

- Cherry tomatoes (0.5 lb.)

- Green beans (1 lb., trimmed and halved)

Directions:

1. Turn the air fryer up to 360 degrees.

2. Combine all of the ingredients into the basket of the air fryer and close the lid to cook.

3. After 20 minutes, divide this between four servings and enjoy.

Nutrition: Calories 174 Carbs 11g Fat 5g Protein 4g

44. Buttery Artichokes

Preparation time: 15 minutes

Cooking time: 20 minutes

Servings: 4

Ingredients:

- Lemon (1 Tablespoon., grated for zest)

- Cumin (0.25 teaspoon, ground)

- Butter (4 Tablespoon., melted)

- Pepper and salt

- Olive oil (1 Tablespoon.)

- Garlic cloves (3, minced)

- Artichokes (4, trimmed)

Directions:

1. Turn on the air fryer and get it to warm up to 370 degrees.

2. Bring out a bowl and add all of the ingredients inside. Toss and move to the air fryer basket to cook.

3. After 20 minutes, this is done. Add to some plates and serve.

Nutrition: Calories 214 Carbs 12g Fat 5g Protein 5g

45. Ginger Mushrooms

Preparation time: 5 minutes

Cooking time: 20 minutes

Servings: 4

Ingredients:

- Pepper and salt

- Ginger (1 Tablespoon., grated)

- White mushrooms (2 lbs., halved)

- Balsamic vinegar (2 Tablespoon.)

- Olive oil (2 Tablespoon.)

Directions:

1. Take all the ingredients and combine them inside the basket of the air fryer.

2. Turn the air fryer on to 360 degrees and put the lid on top to cook.

3. After 20 minutes, take this out and divide before serving.

Nutrition: Calories 182 Carbs 8g Fat 3g Protein 4g

46. Masala Potatoes

Preparation time: 15 minutes

Cooking time: 20 minutes

Servings: 4

Ingredients:

- Salt and pepper

- Juice from one lime

- Garam masala (1 teaspoon)

- Garlic powder (1 teaspoon)

- Olive oil (1 Tablespoon.)

- Gold potatoes (2 lbs., peeled and cubed)

Directions:

1. Turn on the air fryer and let it heat up to 370 degrees.

2. Put the basket into the machine and combine all the ingredients inside of it before adding the lid.

3. After 20 minutes of cooking, divide up the potatoes, and serve.

Nutrition: Calories 182 Carbs 12g Fat 4g Protein 4g

47. <u>Mixed Veggie Chips</u>

Preparation time: 5 minutes

Cooking time: 9 minutes

Servings: 4

Ingredients:

- Cumin powder

- Italian seasoning (1 teaspoon)

- Salt (1 teaspoon.)

- Carrot (1)

- Peeled red beet (1)

- Pepper (0.5 teaspoon)

- Sweet potato (1, peeled)

- Zucchini (1)

Directions:

1. Turn on the air fryer to be at the dehydrate mode at 110 degrees.

2. While that goes on, take a mandolin slicer and slice the vegetables before putting it into a bowl. Season with all the seasonings and toss around.

3. Doing so in batches, arrange these into the air fryer cooking tray and let bake.

4. After seven to nine minutes, the vegetables should be crispy. Move it out of the machine and repeat the batches until done.

Nutrition: Calories 84 Carbs 18g Fat 1g Protein 2g

48. Pear and Apple Chips

Preparation time: 5 minutes

Cooking time: 7 minutes

Servings: 4

Ingredients:

- Pears (6, peeled)

- Honey crisp apples (6)

Directions:

1. Turn on the air fryer to be at the dehydrate mode and reach 110 degrees.

2. Use a slicer to slice up the pears and apples thinly.

3. Doing so in batches, arrange the slices of fruit on the bottom of the air fryer, doing it in one layer.

4. Close the lid and let it cook for a bit. The fruit will be crispy after seven minutes.

5. Repeat until the fruit is cooked and serve.

Nutrition: Calories 142 Carbs 38g Fat 1g Protein 1g

49. Mixed Veggie Salad

Preparation time: 25 minutes

Cooking Time: 1 hour 35 minutes

Servings: 8

Ingredients:

- 2 tablespoons olive oil, divided

- 3 medium zucchinis, sliced into ½-inch thick rounds

- 3 small eggplants, sliced into ½-inch thick rounds

- 4 medium tomatoes, cut in eighths

- 1 cup cherry tomatoes, quartered

- 2 red bell peppers, seeded and chopped

- 4 fresh basil leaves, chopped

- ½ cup Italian dressing

- Salt, as required

- ½ cup Parmesan cheese, grated

Directions:

1. Set the temperature of air fryer to 355 degrees F. Grease an air fryer basket.

2. In a bowl, mix together the zucchini and one tablespoon of oil.

3. Place zucchini slices into the prepared air fryer basket.

4. Air fry for about 25 minutes.

5. Remove from air fryer and place the zucchini slices into a bowl. Set aside.

6. In another bowl, mix well eggplant and one tablespoon of oil.

7. Place eggplant slices into the greased air fryer basket.

8. Air fry for about 30-40 minutes.

9. Remove from air fryer and place the eggplant slices into a bowl with zucchini. Set aside.

10. Now, set the temperature of air fryer to 320 degrees F.

11. Place tomatoes into the greased air fryer basket.

12. Air fry for about 30 minutes.

13. Remove from air fryer and place the tomatoes into a bowl with veggies.

14. In the bowl of cooked vegetables, add the bell pepper, basil, salt, dressing, and salt and gently, stir to combine.

15. Cover the bowl of salad and refrigerate for 2 hours before serving.

16. Garnish with Parmesan cheese and serve.

Nutrition: Calories: 179 Carbohydrate: 21.6g Protein: 6g Fat: 9.6g Sugar: 12.4g Sodium: 83mg

50. <u>Honey Glazed Carrots</u>

Preparation time: 15 minutes

Cooking Time: 12 minutes

Servings: 4

Ingredients:

- 3 cups carrots, peeled and cut into large chunks

- 1 tablespoon olive oil

- 1 tablespoon honey

- 1 tablespoon fresh thyme, finely chopped

- Salt and ground black pepper, as required

Directions:

1. Set the temperature of air fryer to 390 degrees F. Grease an air fryer basket.

2. In a bowl, mix well carrot, oil, honey, thyme, salt, and black pepper.

3. Arrange carrot chunks into the prepared air fryer basket in a single layer.

4. Air fry for about 12 minutes.

5. Remove from air fryer and transfer the carrot chunks onto
    serving plates.

6. Serve hot.

Nutrition: Calories: 82 Carbohydrate: 12.9g Protein: 0.8g Fat: 3.6g

Sugar: 8.4g Sodium: 96mg

30 DAYS MEAL PLAN

Days	Breakfast	Snacks	Dinner
1	Sausage and Egg Breakfast Burrito	Eggplant Mix	Roasted Salmon with Lemon and Rosemary
2	Eggs in Avocado	Garlic Kale	Air Fried Meatballs with Parsley
3	French Toast Sticks	Herbed Tomatoes	Succulent Flank Steak
4	Home-Fried Potatoes	Coriander Potatoes	Chili Roasted Eggplant Soba
5	Homemade Cherry Breakfast Tarts	Tomatoes and Green beans	Quinoa and Spinach Cakes
6	Sausage and Cream Cheese Biscuits	Buttery Artichokes	Air Fried Cajun Shrimp
7	Fried Chicken and Waffles	Ginger Mushrooms	Air Fried Squid Rings
8	Cheesy Tater Tot Breakfast Bake	Masala Potatoes	Marinated Portobello Mushroom
9	Breakfast Scramble Casserole	Mixed Veggie Chips	Air Fried Meatloaf
10	Homemade Cherry Breakfast Tarts	Pear and Apple Chips	Fettuccini with Roasted Vegetables in Tomato Sauce
11	Mozzarella Tots	Banana and Cocoa Chips	Herbed Parmesan Turkey Meatballs
12	Chicken Balls	Roasted Chickpeas	Teriyaki Glazed Salmon and Vegetable Roast
13	Tofu Egg Scramble	Zucchini Chips	Sirloin with Garlic and Thyme
14	Flax & Hemp Porridge	Ranch Garlic Pretzels	Herbed Parmesan Turkey Meatballs

15	Creamy Bacon Eggs	Yellow Squash and Cream Cheese Fritters	Yogurt Garlic Chicken
16	Cheddar Bacon Hash	Air Fry Cheesy Taco Hot dogs	Lemony Parmesan Salmon
17	Cheddar Soufflé with Herbs	Crispy French Toast Sticks	Easiest Tuna Cobbler Ever
18	Bacon Butter Biscuits	Buttered Corn Cob	Deliciously Homemade Pork Buns
19	Keto Parmesan Frittata	Roasted Cashews	Mouthwatering Tuna Melts
20	Chicken Liver Pate	Panko Zucchini Fries	Bacon Wings
21	Coconut Pancake Hash	Rosemary Turnip Chips	Pepper Pesto Lamb
22	Beef Slices	Rosemary Carrot Fries	Tuna Spinach Casserole
23	Flax & Chia Porridge	Butternut Squash Fries	Greek Style Mini Burger Pies
24	Paprika Eggs with Bacon	Breaded Pickle Fries	Family Fun Pizza
25	Quiche Muffin Cups	Buttered Corn Cob	Crispy Hot Sauce Chicken
26	Easy Scotch Eggs	Polenta Bars	Herbed Parmesan Turkey Meatballs
27	Strawberry Toast	Eggplant Crisps	Sweet Potatoes & Creamy Crisp Chicken
28	Cinnamon Sweet-Potato Chips	Roasted Pecans	Mushroom & Chicken Noodles with Glasswort and Sesame
29	Quiche Muffin Cups	Crispy Broccoli Poppers	Prawn Chicken Drumettes
30	Vegetable and Ham Omelet	Potato Cheese Croquettes	Asian Popcorn Chicken

CONCLUSION

With the growing demand for healthier cooking and better nutrition, people have turned to the air fryer as an alternative way of cooking without fat. After all, too much fat from fried foods in one's diet contributes to obesity and cardiovascular diseases. However, fat really does make food palatable. No wonder it's tough to give up that pleasant fried taste. With an air fryer, though, you capture the great taste of fried foods without the use of oil. It's a practical way for anyone striving to become slim and healthy.

Healthy food should not be a fad or an impossibility to choose; it should be part of everyone's life. Of course, this does not mean that you must give up enjoying the kitchen; neither of the many dishes that can be prepared healthy. To get it there are certain appliances that can help you and a lot: for example, an air fryer.

The concept of an air fryer is to fry food items in the air instead of oil. This revolutionary kitchen appliance uses superheated air that circulates to cook the food. This way, you don't have to dunk your food in sizzling hot fat just to achieve that crunch.

Regarding structure, an air fryer almost looks like a large rice cooker but with a front door handle. It has a removable chunky tray that holds the food to the air fried. It has an integrated timer to allow you to pre-set cooking times, and an adjustable temperature control so you can pre-set the best cooking temperature.

Different models offer different features, such as digital displays, auto-power shut-off, but mostly they work the same and use the same technology.

The air fryers have gained a lot of popularity over the last years due to their many advantages. Cooking in an air fryer is such a great and fun experience and you should try it as soon as possible.

The air fryer is such an innovative appliance that allows you to cook some of the best, most succulent and rich meals for you, your family and friends.

CPSIA information can be obtained
at www.ICGtesting.com
Printed in the USA
BVHW061716150421
605030BV00004B/768